UNDERSTANDING ACCOUNTING   Ephraim Unuigbe

ABOUT THE BOOK

"Understanding Accounting for the Non-Accountants" is a course designed to provide a basic understanding of accounting principles and practices for those not trained as accountants. The course covers the fundamental accounting concepts, including the accounting equation, the duality concept, and the steps in the accounting cycle.

In this course, you will learn about the different types of transactions that can occur in a business, including revenue, expenses, assets, liabilities, and equity. You will also learn about the primary financial statements, including the balance sheet, income statement, and statement of cash flows, and how they are used by investors, creditors, and management.

In addition to covering the basics of accounting, this course also emphasizes the importance of ethical behaviour in the accounting profession. You will learn about professional standards and the role of professional organisations in promoting ethical conduct.

By the end of this course, you will have a solid foundation in accounting and be well-equipped to continue learning about this important field. So, whether you are an entrepreneur, a small business owner, or simply interested in gaining a better understanding of accounting, this course is for you.

ABOUT THE AUTHOR

Ephraim Unuigbe holds several credentials, including a BSc in Accounting and membership in the Institute of Chartered Accountants of Nigeria. He is also a Certified Information Systems Auditor, certified by the Information Systems Audit and Control Association. In addition to his background in accounting, Unuigbe is also a certified public speaker and career personal finance coach.

Ephraim is currently employed at one of the leading accounting firms in the United Kingdom, where he is responsible for providing assurance services to corporate clients. In addition to his professional pursuits, Ephraim is also actively involved in the community. He serves as the Director of Corporate Governance on the board of HACTRI, a Nigerian literacy organisation. In addition, he is a board member of Itchen Sixth Form College in the United Kingdom.

Ephraim is married to Marian Unuigbe and has two children, Eseohen Elizabeth and Daniel Chukwudi.

OTHER BOOKS BY THE AUTHOR TO DATE

- Succeeding in your career - A Roadmap for Graduates & Young Professionals

- Let's talk about money - A guide to Personal Finances for Young Adults

- How to choose a career path - A Spiritual Perspective to Career Choice & Life

- Managing Family Finance - for Career Couples

- Career & Romance - How to Find Your Soul Mate as a Single Career Professional

- The Career Woman's Guide to SINGLE PARENTING: For Single Female Career Professionals with teenage kids between the ages of 12 -19.

- Understanding investment for beginners

All available on amazon.com and www.ephraim-unuigbe.online

Contact the author via info@ephraim-unuigbe.online or ephraim.unuigbe@gmail.com

SERVICES WE OFFER

Career Counselling
We assist individuals of all ages in clarifying and attaining their career goals. We also teach students the development of learner-centred so they can utiliutilise their academic careers and life beyond.

Personal Finance Coaching
Personal finance refers to how well people adhere to a budget when managing their finances. Over time, the goal is to save money while also spending money on needed resources and allocating a particular amount for each living expense. With my guidance, you will learn how to make, manage, and multiply your money.

CV Review and Writing
The modern world of employment demands that your CV stands out, and we provide a range of services through which our professional CV writers can create the CV just for you. Every CV we create is tailored specifically to meet your needs.

Cover Letter and Personal Statement
We will provide you with a professional who can write you a high-performing letter for your job application or personal statement. Paired with our professionally written CV, you ca , differentiate yourself from other applicants.

LinkedIn Profile Optimization

You can take your LinkedIn profile to the next level and turn it into a powerful career tool that highlights your abilities and eexperience and impresses your network of contacts.

Interview Coaching

Our professionals help you be the best candidate your potential employer has ever seen. A well-rounded approach that addresses the verbal and non-verbal factors.

Understanding Accounting

for the

NON-ACCOUNTANT

EPHRAIM UNUIGBE (ACA)

Copyright December 2022 © **Ephraim Unuigbe**

All rights reserved.

No part of this book may be reproduced, distributed, stored, or transmitted in any form or by any means, including electronic, photocopy, recording, copying or resale, without the prior written permission of the author and publisher, except in the case of brief quotations embodied in reviews and articles as well as specific other non-commercial uses permitted by copyright law.

Contact the author via info@ephraim-unuigbe.online; ephraim.unuigbe@gmail.com

DEDICATION

To God. Thank you.

TABLE OF CONTENTS

Chapter One - Introduction to Accounting Principles

- The accounting equation
- The duality concepts

Chapter Two - The Accounting Cycle

- Identifying transactions
- Recording transactions in journals
- Posting to ledger accounts
- Preparing a trial balance
- Preparing financial statements

Chapter Three - Financial Statements

- The balance sheets
- The income statements
- The statement of cash flows

Chapter Four - Types of Transactions

- Revenue
- Expenses

- Assets
- Liabilities
- Equity

Chapter Five - Ratios and Analysis

- Introduction to financial ratios
- Common ratios (e.g., P/E ratio, D/E ratio, ROE)

Chapter Six - Ethics in Accounting

- The importance of ethical behaviour in the accounting profession
- Professional standards and professional organisations

Chapter Seven - Conclusion

- Summary of key points
- Encouragement to continue learning about accounting

PREFACE

Welcome to "Understanding Accounting for the Non-Accountants"! This course is designed to provide a basic understanding of accounting principles and practices for those who need to be trained as accountants.

Accounting is a required field that plays a vital role in business. It is the language of business and is used to communicate financial information to a wide range of stakeholders, including investors, creditors, and management.

Whether you are an entrepreneur, a small business owner, or simply interested in learning more about accounting, this course is for you. We will cover the accounting basics, including the accounting equation and the duality concept, the steps in the accounting cycle, the primary financial statements, and the different types of transactions that can occur. We will also discuss the importance of ethical behaviour in the accounting profession and the role of professional organisations in promoting ethical standards.

By the end of this course, you will have a solid foundation in accounting and be well-equipped to continue learning about this important field. So whether you want to start your own business or gain a better understanding of counting works, this course is an excellent starting point.

I hope you enjoy this course on "Understanding Accounting for Non-Accountants"! Let's get started.

CHAPTER ONE

INTRODUCTION TO ACCOUNTING PRINCIPLES

Accounting is the process of recording, classifying, and summarizing financial transactions to provide helpful information in business decisions. To understand accounting, it is important to familiarize yourself with some basic principles that govern the field.

The Accounting Equation

The accounting equation, one of the foundation principles in accounting, states that assets are equal to the sum of liabilities and equity. It is important to note that this equation is always balanced, meaning that any change in one component must be reflected by a corresponding change in the other components.

The accounting equation says that a company's assets (things it owns) are equal to its liabilities (debts it owes) plus its equity (the amount of money it has left after paying off its debts). This equation always has to balance out, which means that if something changes on one side, something else has to switch on the other side to make it even.

For example, if a company purchases a new piece of equipment, its assets will increase by the cost of the equipment, and its equity will also increase by the same amount. This is because the company has used its own funds (equity) to purchase the asset. On the other hand, if the company takes on a loan to finance the purchase, its assets will increase by the cost of the equipment, but its liabilities will also increase by the amount of the loan.

Here's an example: if a company buys a new computer for $1,000, it will increase its assets (the computer is now something it owns) by $1,000. In addition, its equity will also increase by $1,000 because it used its own computer. But if the company takes out a loan to buy the computer instead, its assets will still go up by $1,000 (because it has the computer), but its liabilities (debts it owes) will also go up by $1,000 (because it has a loan to pay back).

The Duality Concept

Another important principle in accounting is the duality concept, which states that every financial transaction has two equal and opposite effects on the accounting equation. This is because every transaction involves at least two accounts, one debited (increased) and one credited (decreased).

The duality concept is another important principle in accounting. It says that every financial transaction affects at least two different parts of the accounting equation in equal but opposite ways.

For example, when a company sells something to a customer, it will increase the amount of money it has (called revenue) and decreases the amount of stuff it has in stock (called inventory). This is because the company got money in exchange for something it no longer has.

Here's another example: if a company pays its rent for the month, it will decrease its assets (the money it has on hand) and increase its liabilities (the debts it owes). Again, this is because it is using its own money to pay off a debt.

The accounting equation and the duality concept are two basic principles form the accounting foundation.

By understanding these principles, you will be better equipped to understand the financial transactions of a business and how they are reported in the financial statements.

One of these principles is the accounting equation. It states that assets are equal to liabilities plus equity. This means that all the assets a company has are equal to the amount of money it owes to others (liabilities) and the amount of money that belongs to the owners (equity). This equation is always balanced, which means that any changes in one part of the equation must also be reflected in the other parts. This helps ensure that all financial transactions are accurately recorded and tracked.

There are many other accounting principles in addition to the accounting equation and the duality concept. Here are a few more principles with simplified explanations and examples:

1. The going concern principle assumes that a business will continue to operate indefinitely rather than being closed or liquidated in the near future. This assumption allows companies to record assets and liabilities at their current value rather than their liquidation value. For example, a company's building may be worth more if the business is expected to continue using it for the foreseeable future than if the business were to close down and sell the building.

2. The consistency principle requires companies to use the same accounting methods from one period to the next. This allows a better comparison of financial statements from one period to the next. For example, if a company changes how it calculates the depreciation of its equipment, it won't be easy to compare the

financial statements from one year to the next because the expenses will be reported differently.

3. The materiality principle states that material (important) information should be disclosed in financial statements, while immaterial (unimportant) information can be omitted. The threshold for what is considered material varies depending on the size and complexity of the business. For example, a small business may consider a $500 error material, while a large multinational corporation may consider a $500,000 error immaterial.

4. The objectivity principle requires financial information to be based on objective evidence rather than subjective judgment. This helps to ensure that the financial statements are reliable and trustworthy. For example, a company should record the sale of goods at the actual

selling price rather than an inflated price based on the company's subjective assessment of the value of the goods.

5. The full disclosure principle requires companies to disclose all relevant information in financial statements. This includes not only information that is required by accounting standards but also any additional information that might be useful to users of the financial statements. For example, a company might need to disclose information about a lawsuit that could significantly impact its financial performance.

summary

Accounting principles are the guidelines and rules that govern the preparation of financial statements. These principles provide a framework for consistent financial reporting and help ensure that financial statements are reliable and accurate.

Several principles are commonly used in accounting, including the following:

The accounting equation: The accounting equation states that a company's assets must equal the sum of its liabilities and equity. In other words, the value of what a company owns (its assets) must be equal to the value of what it owes (its liabilities) plus the value of the owner's interest in the company (its equity). The accounting equation can be written as: Assets = Liabilities + Equity

The duality concept: The duality concept states that every financial transaction has two equal and opposite effects on the accounting equation. For example, when a company buys a new asset, it increases its assets and liabilities or equity, depending on how the asset was financed. This concept helps ensure that the accounting equation remains in the balance after every transaction.

CHAPTER TWO

THE ACCOUNTING CYCLE

This chapter outlines the steps in the accounting cycle, including identifying transactions, recording transactions in journals, posting to ledger accounts, preparing a trial balance, and preparing financial statements.

The accounting cycle is the process of recording and organizing a company's financial information. It is an essential part of running a business, as it helps to ensure that financial transactions are recorded accurately and consistently. Here is a more detailed look at the steps in the accounting cycle:

Identifying transactions

The first step in the accounting cycle is to identify the financial transactions that have occurred. This includes identifying the sources of the transactions (such as customers, suppliers, or employees), as well as the types of transactions (such as sales, purchases, or salaries).

Identifying transactions also involves reviewing documents such as invoices, receipts, and bank statements to determine which transactions need to be recorded. Again, it is important to be thorough in this step, as any missed transactions will not be reflected in the financial statements. This can lead to inaccurate financial reports and may impact decision-making within the company.

Here are some examples of transactions that may need to be identified:

- Sales: When a company sells goods or services to customers actions, this transaction needs to be recorded. The invoice or receipt provided by the company to the customer is evidence of the sale and should be used to identify the transaction.

- Purchases: When a company buys goods or services from a supplier, this transaction needs to be recorded. The invoice or receipt provided by the supplier to the company is evidence of the purchase and should be used to identify the transaction.

- Payments: When a company makes or receives a payment, this is a transaction that needs to be recorded. Bank statements and cash register records can be used to identify payments made or received by the company.

By carefully reviewing these and other documents, the accountant can identify all the transactions that have occurred and ensure that they are properly recorded in the accounting records.

Recording transactions in journals

Once the transactions have been identified, they must be recorded in the appropriate journal. A journal is a record of a business's financial tran, organized by type. There are several different types of journals, including the sales journal, the cash receipts journal, and the purchases journal. Each journal is used to record a specific type of transaction.

For example, the sales journal is used to record records all sales transactions, and the cash receipts journal is used to record all cash payments received by the business. Likewise, the purchases journal is used to record all purchases made by the business, and the cash payments journal is used to record all cash payments made by the business.

To record a transaction in a journal, the accountant will enter the transaction details in the journal, including the date, the type of transaction, the account affected, and the amount of the transaction. For example, if a company sells goods to a customer for $100, the accountant will record the transaction in the sales journal as follows:

Date	Transaction type	Account Affected	Amount
Jan 1	Sales	Revenue	$100

This entry would show that on January 1, the company made a sale of $100

Journal entries consist of debits and credits to the appropriate accounts. A debit is an increase in an asset account or a decrease in a liability or equity account, while a credit is a decrease in an asset account or an increase in a liability or equity account.

Posting to ledger accounts:

After the transactions have been recorded in the journals, they must be posted to the appropriate ledger accounts. A ledger is a record of a business's financial transactions organized by account. There are several ledger accounts, including accounts receivable, accounts payable, and cash. Each ledger account is used to track a specific type.

For example, the accounts receivable ledger is used to track the money that is owed to the business by its customers. The accounts payable ledger is used to track the money that the business owes to its suppliers. The cash ledger is used to track the company's cash inflows and outflows.

The accountant would then transfer this information to the Sales ledger account, where the $100 sale would be recorded as a debit, and the Accounts Receivable ledger account, where the $100 would be recorded as a credit. This process is known as posting, and it is an essential step in the accounting cycle as it allows for accurate and organized record-keeping of financial transactions. This way, the accountant can easily track a company's financial performance and make informed decisions about the business.

Date	Transaction Type	Account Affected	Amount
Jan 1	Sales	Revenue	$100

To post this transaction to the ledger, the accountant would transfer the information to the revenue account in the ledger like this:

Account	Date	Transaction Type	Amount
Revenue	Jan 1	Sales	$100

This entry would show that on January 1, the company had a sale of $100 and that the revenue account was increased by $100.

Preparing a trial balance:

After all the transactions have been recorded in the ledger accounts, a trial balance can be prepared. A trial balance is a list of all the accounts in the ledger and the balances in each. The trial balance is used to ensure that the debits and credits in the ledger are in balance, indicating that the transactions have been recorded correctly.

To prepare a trial balance, the accountant will first list all the accounts in the ledger and their balances. Then, the chances of each account will be taken from the ledger and show either a debit or a credit balance, depending on the nature of the account. For example, accounts that typically have a debit balance include accounts payable and expenses, while accounts that typically have a credit balance include revenue and equity.

Once all the balances have been listed, the accountant will add up all the debit balances and all the credit balances separately. If the total debits equal the total credits, the ledger is in balance and the transactions have been recorded correctly. If the totals do not maHowever, ifh, it may indicate an error in the ledger, and the accountant will need to investigate further to find and correct the error.

Preparing financial statements

Once the trial balance has been prepared, the financial statements can be prepared. There are three primary financial statements: the balance sheet, which shows the financial position of the business at a specific point in time; the income statement, which shows the financial performance of the business over a period of time; and the statement of cash flows, which shows the cash inflows and outflows of the business over a period of time.

The balance sheet is a snapshot of a company's financial position at a specific point in time. It shows the company's assets, liabilities, and equity. The assets are the company's resources, such as cash, inventory, and equipment. The liabilities are the debts the company owes, such as loans and accounts payable. Finally, equity is the difference between the assets and liabilities and represents the owners' interest in the company.

The income statement shows the company's financial performance over a period of time, such as a month or a year. It shows the company's revenue and expenses and the net income or loss for the period. The net income is the difference between the revenue and the expenses and represents the company's profitability.

The statement of cash flows shows the company's cash inflows and outflows over a period of time. It separates the cash flows into three categories: operating activities, investing activities, and financing activities. The operating activities include the cash flows related to the company's core operations, such as sales and expenses. The investing activities include the cash flows related to the company's investments in long-term assets, such as equipment or real estate. The financing activities include the cash flows related to the company's financing, such as borrowing or repaying debt.

Summary

The accounting cycle is the process of recording, classifying, and summarizing financial transactions to provide useful information in business decisions. The cycle consists of the following steps:

Identifying transactions: The first step in the accounting cycle is to identify the financial transactions that have occurred. This includes reviewing documents such as invoices, receipts, and bank statements to determine which transactions need to be recorded.

Recording transactions in journals: Once the transactions have been identified, they must be recorded in the appropriate journal. A journal is a record of a business's financial transactions, organized by type. There are several different types of journals, including the sales journal, the cash receipts journal, and the purchases journal.

Posting to ledger accounts: After the transactions have been recorded in the journals, they must be posted to the appropriate ledger accounts. A ledger is a record of a business's financial transactions organized by account. There are several tedger accounts, including accounts receivable, accounts payable, and cash.

Preparing a trial balance: After all the transactions have been recorded in the ledger accounts, a trial balance can be prepared. A trial balance is a list of all the accounts in the ledger and the balances in each. It is used to ensure that the debits and credits in the ledger are in balance, indicating that the transactions have been recorded correctly.

Preparing financial statements: Once the trial balance has been prepared, the financial statements can be prepared. There are three main financial statements: the balance sheet, which shows the financial position of the business at a specific point in time; the income statement, which shows the financial performance of the business over a period of time; and the statement of cash flows, which shows the cash inflows and outflows of the business over a period of time.

CHAPTER THREE

FINANCIAL STATEMENTS

This chapter describes the main financial statements, including the balance sheet, income statement, and statement of cash flows. Explain the purpose of each statement and how they are used by investors, creditors, and management.

Financial Statements: An Overview

Financial statements provide information about a company's financial performance and position. They are used by investors, creditors, and management to make informed decisions about the company. There are three main financial statements: the balance sheet, the income statement, and the statement of cash flows.

The Balance Sheet

The balance sheet is a snapshot of a company's financial position at a specific time. It shows the company's assets, liabilities, and equity.

Assets are a company's resources, such as cash, inventory, and equipment. A company's liabilities are debts, such as loans and accounts payable. Equity is the difference between assets and liabilities and represents the owners' interest in the company.

The balance sheet is helpful for understanding the financial strength of a company. It can help investors and creditors assess the company's ability to pay its debts and generate profits. It can also help management identify areas of the business that may need improvement.

Here is an example of a balance sheet:

Balance Sheets

Assets	Liabilities	Equity
Cash	Accounts Payable	Common Stock
Inventory	Loans	Retained Earnings
Equipment		

In this example, the company has $100 in cash, $200 in inventory, and $300 in equipment for a total of $600 in assets. It also has $100 in accounts payable and $200 in loans for a total of $300 in liabilities. The equity is $300, which is the difference between the assets and liabilities.

The Income Statement

The income statement shows the company's financial performance over a period of time, such as a month or a year. It shows the company's revenue and expenses, and the net income or loss for the period.

Revenue is the money that a company earns from selling goods or services. Expenses are the costs that a company incurs in order to generate revenue, such as the cost of goods sold, salaries, and rent. The net income is the difference between the revenue and the expenses and represents the company's profitability.

The income statement is helpful for understanding the financial performance of a company. It can help investors and creditors assess the company's ability to generate profits and manage expenses. It can also help management identify areas of the business that may need to be more efficient or in need of improvement.

Here is an example of an income statement:

Income Statement

Revenue	Expenses	Net Income
$1,000	$500	$500

In this example, the company had revenue of $1,000 and expenses of $500, resulting in a net income of $500.

The Statement of Cash Flows

The statement of cash flows shows the company's cash inflows and outflows over a period of time. It separates the cash flows into three categories: operating activities, investing activities, and financing activities.

Operating activities include the cash flows related to the company's core operations, such as sales and expenses.

Investing activities include the cash flows related to the company's investments in long-term assets, such as equipment or real estate.

Financing activities include the cash flows related to the company's financing, such as borrowing or repaying debt.

The statement of cash flows is helpful for understanding the sources and uses of a company's cash. It can help investors and creditors assess the company's ability to generate cash and manage its cash flow. It can also help management identify areas of the business that may be affecting the company's cash position.

Here is an example of a statement of cash flows:

Statement of Cash Flows

Activity	Cash Inflows	Cash Outflows	Net Change in Cash
Operating	$1,000	$500	$500
Investing	$0	$200	-$200
Financing	$100	$50	$50
Total	$1,100	$750	$350
Operating			
Investing			
- Purchase of equipment		$200	
Financing			
- Loans received	$100		
- Repayment of loans		$50	

In this example, the company had cash inflows from operating activities of $1,000 and cash outflows from operating activities of $500, resulting in a net change in cash of $500. It also had cash outflows from investing activities of $200 for the purchase of equipment, cash inflows from financing activities of

$100 from loans received, and cash outflows from financing activities of $50 for the repayment of loans, resulting in a net change in cash of $50.

Use of the financial statements

Financial statements are used by investors, creditors, and management to make informed decisions about a company. Here's how they are used:

Investors: Investors use financial statements to evaluate a company's financial health and determine whether it is a good investment. They may look at the balance sheet to assess the company's assets, liabilities, and equity and the income statement to evaluate the company's profitability. They may also look at the statement of cash flows to understand the company's cash inflows and outflows and assess its ability to generate cash.

Creditors: Creditors, such as banks and other lenders, use financial statements to determine whether to lend money to a company and, if so, how much to lend and at what terms. They may look at the balance sheet to assess the company's ability to pay its debts and the income statement to evaluate the company's profitability. They may also look at the statement of cash flows to understand the company's cash inflows and outflows and assess its ability to generate cash.

Management: Management uses financial statements to make informed decisions about the company's operations and strategic direction. They may look at the balance sheet to assess the company's financial position and identify areas of the business that may need improvement. They may also look at the income statement to evaluate the company's profitability and identify areas of the business that may be inefficient or in need of improvement. The statement of cash flows can also be useful for management in understanding the sources and uses of the company's cash and in forecasting future cash needs.

In addition to using financial statements to make informed decisions, management is also responsible for preparing and presenting financial statements that accurately reflect the company's financial position and performance. This requires adhering to generally accepted accounting principles (GAAP) or International Financial Reporting Standards (IFRS) and ensuring that the financial statements are complete and accurate.

Summary

Financial statements provide information about a company's financial performance and position. They are used by investors, creditors, and management to make informed decisions about the company. There are three main financial statements:

The balance sheet: The balance sheet is a snapshot of a company's financial position at a specific time. It shows the company's assets, liabilities, and equity.

The income statement: The income statement shows the company's financial performance over a period of time, such as a month or a year. It shows the company's revenue and expenses and the net income or loss for the period.

The statement of cash flows: The statement of cash flows shows the company's cash inflows and outflows over a period of time. It separates the cash flows into three categories: operating activities, investing activities, and financing activities.

Financial statements serve as a valuable resource for both internal and external parties. They provide insight into a company's financial health and performance, allowing investors and creditors to evaluate the organization's strength and stability. Additionally, management can use these statements to inform decision-making and guide the company's strategic direction. Financial statements are compiled in accordance with Generally Accepted Accounting Principles (GAAP) or International Financial Reporting Standards (IFRS) to ensure accuracy and consistency.

CHAPTER FOUR

TYPES OF TRANSACTIONS

Discuss the different types of transactions, including revenue, expenses, assets, liabilities, and equity. Explain how these transactions are recorded and reported in the financial statements.

In accounting, transactions are events that financially impact a business. These transactions can be classified into several categories, including revenue, expenses, assets, liabilities, and equity. Understanding these different types of transactions is important for accurately recording and reporting financial information.

Revenue

Revenue is the money that a company earns from selling goods or services. It is recorded as a credit in the income statement and increases the company's equity.

For example, if a company sells goods for $100, the transaction would be recorded as follows:

Date	Transaction type	Account Affected	Amount
Jan 1	Sales	Revenue	$100

This entry would show that on January 1, the company had a sale of $100 and that the revenue account was increased by $100.

Expenses

Expenses are the costs that a company incurs in order to generate revenue. They are recorded as a debit in the income statement and decrease the company's equity.

For example, if a company incurs $50 in costs to produce goods that it sells, the transaction would be recorded as follows:

Date	Transaction Type	Account Affected	Amount
Jan 1	Cost of Goods Sold	Expense	$50

This entry would show that on January 1, the company incurred a cost of $50 and that the expense account was increased by $50.

Assets

Assets are the resources that a company owns. They can be tangible, such as cash, inventory, and equipment, or intangible, such as patents and trademarks. Assets are recorded as a debit in the balance sheet and increase the company's assets.

For example, if a company buys equipment for $100, the transaction would be recorded as follows:

Date	Transaction Type	Account Affected	Amount
Jan 1	Purchase of Equipment	Equipment	$100

This entry would show that on January 1, the company purchased equipment for $100 and increased the equipment account by $100.

Liabilities

Liabilities are the debts that a company owes. They can be short-term, such as accounts payable, or long-term, such as loans. Liabilities are recorded as a credit in the balance sheet, increasing the company's liabilities.

For example, if a company borrows $100 from a bank, the transaction would be recorded as follows:

Date	Transaction Type	Account Affected	Amount
Jan 1	Loan from Bank	Loans	$100

This entry would show that on January 1, the company borrowed $100 from the bank and that the loans account was increased by $100.

Equity

Equity represents the owners' interest in a company. It is the difference between the company's assets and liabilities and is recorded as a credit in the balance sheet. Equity can be increased by contributions from the owners or by the company's profits. It can be decreased by the company's losses or by distributions to the owners.

For example, if a company has assets of $500 and liabilities of $200, the equity would be $300 (assets of $500 minus liabilities of $200).

These are the main types of transactions that can occur in accounting. Understanding how these transactions are recorded and reported in the financial statements is important for accurately presenting the financial position and performance of a company.

Summary

In accounting, transactions are events that financially impact a business. These transactions can be classified into several categories:

- Revenue: Revenue is a company's money from selling goods or services. It is recorded as a credit in the income statement and increases the company's equity.
- Expenses: Expenses are the costs that a company incurs in order to generate revenue. They are recorded as a debit in the income statement and decrease the company's equity.
- Assets: Assets are the resources that a company owns. They can be tangible, such as cash, inventory, and equipment, or intangible, such as patents and trademarks. Assets are recorded as a debit in the balance sheet and increase the company's assets.

- Liabilities: Liabilities are the debts that a company owes. They can be short-term, such as accounts payable, or long-term, such as loans. Liabilities are recorded as a credit in the balance sheet, increasing the company's liabilities.
- Equity: Equity represents the owners' interest in a company. The difference between the company's assets and liabilities is recorded as a credit in the balance sheet. Equity can be increased by contributions from the owners or by the company's profits. It can be decreased by the company's losses or by distributions to the owners.

Understanding these different types of transactions is important for accurately recording and reporting financial information.

CHAPTER FIVE

FINANCIAL RATIOS AND ANALYSIS

Financial ratios can be used to analyze a company's financial performance. They are calculated by dividing one financial metric by another and provide a way to compare a company's performance to industry benchmarks or to its own historical performance.

Many different financial ratios can be used to analyze a company's financial performance. Some common ratios include:

- Price-to-Earnings Ratio (P/E Ratio): The P/E ratio is calculated by dividing the company's stock price by its earnings per share (EPS). It indicates the price investors are willing to pay for each dollar of the company's earnings. A higher P/E ratio may indicate that investors expect the company's earnings to grow.

To calculate the P/E ratio, you need to know the company's stock price and its earnings per share (EPS). For example, if a company's stock price is $50 and its EPS is $5, its P/E ratio would be 10 (50/5). This means that investors are willing to pay $10 for each dollar of the company's earnings.

- Debt-to-Equity Ratio (D/E Ratio): The D/E ratio is calculated by dividing the company's total debt by its total equity. It measures the proportion of a company's financing that comes from debt versus equity. A higher D/E ratio may indicate that the company is more reliant on borrowing to finance its operations.

To calculate the D/E ratio, you need to know the company's total debt and equity. For example, if a company has total debt of $100 and total equity of $200, its D/E ratio would be 0.5 (100/200). The company's financing is split evenly between debt and equity.

- Return on Equity (ROE): ROE is calculated by dividing the company's net income by its total equity. It measures the profitability of a company in relation to the equity invested in it. A higher ROE may indicate that the company is generating more profits for its shareholders.
To calculate the ROE, you need to know the company's net income and its total equity. For example, if a company has net income of $50 and total equity of $100, its ROE would be 50% (50/100). This means that the company is generating a 50% return on the equity invested in it.

These are just a few examples of financial ratios that can be used to analyze a company's financial performance. Many other ratios can be useful depending on the specific goals of the analysis.

Using financial ratios to analyze a company's financial performance can be a helpful way to understand the strengths and weaknesses of the business. For example, a company with a high P/E ratio may be seen as a growth opportunity, while a company with a high D/E ratio.

Here are some additional financial ratios that can be used to analyze a company's financial performance:

- Gross Profit Margin: The gross profit margin is calculated by dividing the company's gross profit by its total revenue. It measures the percentage of revenue left after accounting for the cost of goods sold. A higher gross profit margin may indicate that the company is able to sell its products at a higher markup.

- Operating Profit Margin: The operating profit margin is calculated by dividing the company's operating profit by its total revenue. It measures the percentage of revenue left after accounting for the company's operating expenses. A higher operating profit margin may indicate that the company is able to operate more efficiently.

- Net Profit Margin: The net profit margin is calculated by dividing the company's net income by its total revenue. It measures the percentage of revenue left after accounting for all expenses, including taxes. A higher net profit margin may indicate that the company is able to generate a higher return on its sales.

- Current Ratio: The current ratio is calculated by dividing the company's current assets by its current liabilities. It measures the company's ability to pay its short-term debts. A higher current ratio may indicate the company's strong liquidity position.

- Quick Ratio: The quick ratio is similar to the current ratio, but it excludes inventory from the calculation of current assets. This ratio measures the company's ability to pay its short-term debts using only its most liquid assets. A higher quick ratio may indicate that the company has a strong liquidity position even if it has a large inventory.

Summary

Financial ratios can be used to analyze a company's financial performance. They are calculated by dividing one financial metric by another and provide a way to compare a company's performance to industry benchmarks or to its own historical performance.

Many different financial ratios can be used to analyze a company's financial performance, including the price-to-earnings ratio, the debt-to-equity ratio, and the return on equity. Other financial ratios include the gross profit margin, the operating profit margin, the net profit margin, the current ratio, and the quick ratio.

Understanding and using financial ratios can be a helpful way to understand the strengths and weaknesses of a company and make informed decisions about its financial performance.

CHAPTER SIX

ETHICS IN ACCOUNTING

This chapter discusses the importance of ethical behaviour in the accounting profession, including the concept of professional standards and the role of professional organizations.

Ethics is the study of what is right and wrong in human behaviour. In the accounting profession, it is important for professionals to adhere to ethical standards in order to maintain the trust and confidence of their clients and the public.

One way that accounting professionals can ensure that they are acting ethically is by following professional standards. Professional standards are guidelines that outline the behaviour that is expected of professionals in a particular field. In the accounting profession, these standards are set by professional organizations such as the Financial Accounting Standards Board (FASB) and the American Institute of Certified Public Accountants (AICPA).

Professional organizations also play a role in promoting ethical behaviour in the accounting profession. These organizations often have codes of conduct that outline the ethical standards that their members are expected to follow. In addition, professional organizations often provide resources and training to help their members understand and adhere to ethical standards.

Examples of ethical behavior in the accounting profession include:

- Maintaining confidentiality: Accounting professionals are often entrusted with sensitive financial information. It is important for them to keep this information confidential and not share it with others without proper authorization.
- Being objective: Accounting professionals should not allow their personal biases or interests to influence their work. They should remain objective and report information accurately and fairly.
- Avoiding conflicts of interest: Accounting professionals should not allow their personal interests to conflict with their professional duties. For example, they should not accept gifts or favours from clients that could influence their judgement.
- Adhering to professional standards: Accounting professionals should follow the professional standards set by their organization and strive to

maintain the highest level of professional integrity.

- Disclosing all relevant information: Accounting professionals should disclose all relevant information that could impact their work or their clients' financial statements. This includes disclosing any potential biases or limitations in their work.
- Being honest and transparent: Accounting professionals should be honest and transparent in their work and communication with clients and other stakeholders.
- Keeping up-to-date with professional developments: Accounting professionals should stay up-to-date with developments in their field and continue to educate themselves in order to provide the best possible service to their clients.
- Being accountable for their actions: Accounting professionals should be accountable for their

actions and take responsibility for any mistakes they may make.

- Seeking guidance when needed: If an accounting professional is faced with an ethical dilemma or is unsure of the appropriate course of action, they should seek guidance from their professional organization or colleagues.
- Protecting the public interest: Accounting professionals have a responsibility to protect the public interest and act in the best interests of their clients and stakeholders.
- Maintaining independence: In order to maintain the integrity of their work, accounting professionals should be independent and not allow outside influences to affect their judgement.
- Being respectful: Accounting professionals should respect the confidentiality and privacy of their clients and treat them with dignity and respect.

- Being fair: Accounting professionals should be fair in their work and not discriminate against anyone based on their race, gender, religion, age, or other personal characteristics.
- Being reliable: Accounting professionals should be reliable and consistently deliver high quality work to their clients.
- Protecting the reputation of the profession: Accounting professionals should act in a way that protects the reputation of the accounting profession and promotes trust and confidence in the industry.
- Being aware of cultural differences: Accounting professionals should be aware of cultural differences and respect the cultural norms of their clients and colleagues.
- Being responsible for their work: Accounting professionals should be responsible for their work and ensure that it is accurate and meets the required standards.

- Complying with laws and regulations: Accounting professionals should comply with all relevant laws and regulations, including those related to financial reporting, tax, and professional conduct.
- Being respectful of diversity: Accounting professionals should be respectful of diversity and inclusion and strive to create a welcoming and inclusive environment for all.
- Protecting the environment: Accounting professionals should consider the environmental impacts of their work and strive to minimize any adverse effects.

By following these ethical guidelines, accounting professionals can ensure that they are acting with integrity and maintaining the trust of their clients and the public.

Summary

Ethics in accounting refers to the principles and standards of behaviour that guide the actions of accounting professionals. Ethical behaviour in the accounting profession is important in order to maintain the trust and confidence of clients and the public. Some examples of ethical behaviour in the accounting profession include maintaining confidentiality, being objective and honest, avoiding conflicts of interest, adhering to professional standards, and seeking guidance when needed.

Other examples include protecting the public interest, maintaining independence, being respectful, being fair, being reliable, protecting the reputation of the profession, being aware of cultural differences, being responsible for their work, complying with laws and regulations, promoting integrity, being respectful of diversity, protecting the environment, and being responsible for their own professional development. It is important for accounting professionals to adhere to these ethical principles in order to maintain the integrity of their work and the trust of their clients and the public.

CHAPTER SEVEN

CONCLUSION

This chapter summarize the key points covered in the outline and encourage the reader to continue learning about accounting.

In this outline, we have covered the basics of accounting, including the accounting equation and the duality concept, the steps in the accounting cycle, the main financial statements, and the different types of transactions that can occur. We have also discussed the importance of ethical behaviour in the accounting profession and the role of professional organizations in promoting ethical standards.

By understanding these concepts, you will have a strong foundation in accounting and be well-prepared to continue learning about this important field. The world of accounting is constantly evolving, so it is important to continue learning and staying up-to-date on the latest developments.

There are many resources available to help you continue your learning journey in accounting. Professional organizations, such as the American Association of Finance and Accounting (AAFA), the Chartered Institute of Management Accountants (CIMA), the Institute of Chartered Accountants in England and Wales (ICAEW), American Institute of Certified Public Accountants (AICPA), The Institute of Internal Auditors (IIA), Institute of Management Accountants (IMA), Professional Association of Small Business Accountants (PASBA), or Association of Chartered Certified Accountants (ACCA) offer a wide range of resources and training opportunities. In addition, many online courses, books, and other resources can help deepen your understanding of accounting.

This outline has provided a helpful introduction to accounting for non-accountants. We encourage you to continue learning about this fascinating field and to consider pursuing further study or professional development in accounting.

ACKNOWLEDGEMENT

To my most important companion, counselor, helper, intercessor, advocate, strengthener, and standby, the Holy Spirit. Thank you.

www.ingramcontent.com/pod-product-compliance
Lightning Source LLC
Chambersburg PA
CBHW070303220526
45465CB00004B/1722